CW00546721

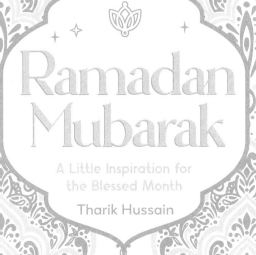

# Ramadan Mubarak

A Little Inspiration for
the Blessed Month

Tharik Hussain

summersdale

RAMADAN MUBARAK

An Hachette UK Company
www.hachette.co.uk

Summersdale Publishers Ltd
Part of Octopus Publishing Group Limited
Carmelite House
50 Victoria Embankment
LONDON
EC4Y 0DZ
UK

www.summersdale.com

Printed and bound in Poland

ISBN: 978-1-83799-134-1

Substantial discounts on bulk quantities of Summersdale books are available to corporations, professional associations and other organizations. For details contact general enquiries: telephone: +44 (0) 1243 771107 or email: enquiries@summersdale.com.

Honorifics for Allah/God (ﷻ) and the Prophet (ﷺ) have not been used in quotes throughout this book if the original quote did not contain them. This is to ensure every quote is as accurate as possible.

# THE SIGNIFICANCE OF RAMADAN

The Qur'an was revealed in Ramadan, when Allah (ﷻ) first spoke to the Prophet Muhammad (ﷺ) on Laylat al-Qadr (the Night of Power). The sacred month also witnessed the Muslim community's first victory in the Battle of Badr, as well as the Prophet's (ﷺ) triumphant return to Makkah.

To fast is better
for you, if only
you knew.

**Qur'an 2:184**

Every deed of the son of Adam is for him, except for fasting. It is for Me and I will reward it.

**Hadith (al-Bukhari)**

He made fasting a citadel
and a shelter for His friends,
opened to them thereby
the gates of Heaven.

Al Ghazali

Fasting had always been a means
of purification for all souls who
longed for divine guidance.

*Aisha Rafea*

# Why Fast?

All the great religions of the world
encourage some form of fasting. While
practices may differ, the underlying
principles often revolve around the
themes of spiritual growth, detoxification,
self-discipline, humility and overall
well-being. It is an ancient wisdom that
can enhance empathy, mental clarity
and awareness of the Divine.

Your Lord will extend His mercy to you and accommodate you in your ordeal.

Qur'an 18:16

Make yourselves
accessible to
God's graces.

Hadith (at-Tabarani)

Verily, fasting is not only
from eating and drinking.
Rather, fasting is from
vanity and obscenity.

Hadith (Ibn Hibban)

Successful indeed is the one

who purifies their soul.

*Qur'an 91:9*

# THE MONTH OF POWER

According to Islamic tradition, Ramadan is a special month when revelations were bestowed on various prophets. It is believed that during Ramadan, the Qur'an was revealed to Muhammad (ﷺ), the Gospel to Isa (Jesus عليه السلام), the Torah to Musa (Moses عليه السلام) and the scriptures to Ibrahim (Abraham عليه السلام). This is no ordinary month.

When My servants
ask you O Prophet
about Me: I am
truly near.

**Qur'an 2:186**

If he comes to
Me walking, I go
to him running.

**Hadith (al-Bukhari)**

I wish I could show you,
when you are lonely or in
darkness, The Astonishing
Light of your own Being!

Hafez

*Sabr** is not to suppress pain.

Grief is a natural part of life.

*Yasmin Mogahed*

\* *sabr* meaning patience and
perseverance in times of adversity

# Conscious of the Lonely

When we belong to large Muslim families
and communities, it is easy to forget that many
Muslims experience solitude. Those new to
Islam may find themselves waking to eat
*suhoor*\* alone and preparing *iftar*\*\* for one.
Theirs is a Ramadan struggle greater
than yours, so reach out to them.

\* *suhoor* meaning the light pre-dawn
meal eaten by those preparing
to fast for the day

\*\* *iftar* meaning the meal eaten
at sunset to break the fast

O ye who believe!
Fasting is prescribed to
you as it was prescribed
to those before you,
that ye may (learn)
self-restraint.

Qur'an 2:183

When the month of
Ramadan starts the
gates of Heaven
are opened.

Hadith (al-Bukhari)

Do not take pleasure
in that which perishes,
and do not anguish over
that which vanishes.

A'isha al-Hiri of Nishapur

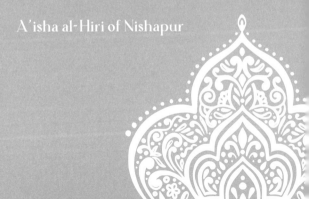

Whosoever rises above things of this world, in front of which you kneel, is much stronger than you.

*Ibn Hazm*

## WHAT ARE MY ATTACHMENTS?

Ramadan is primarily a time for denouncing the *dunya* – the material things we find ourselves so attached to, it causes us distress when we are separated from them. Reflect on what these attachments are in your own life, and how you might also fast from them this Ramadan.

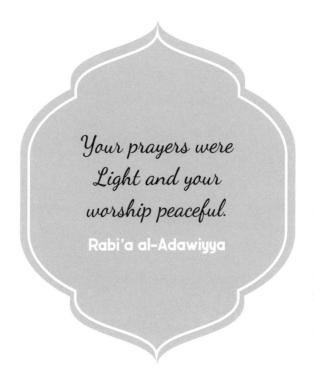

*Your prayers were Light and your worship peaceful.*

**Rabi'a al-Adawiyya**

# A kind word is charity.

## Hadith (al-Bukhari)

And be kind to parents,
relatives, orphans, the poor,
near and distant neighbours,
close friends, needy travellers
and those "bondspeople"
in your possession.

Qur'an 4:36

I have joined what I consider
to be the biggest and best
family in the world.

*Yvonne Ridley*

# The Prophetic Character: Kindness

Kindness is easy, free, yet profoundly impactful. Consider those among Allah's (ﷻ) creations you don't normally think to show kindness to, or always seem too busy for. Whether it's the bus driver on your commute, the thirsty dog you pass each morning or a neglected plant, strive to expand your compassion to them.

And seek help
through patience
and prayer.

Qur'an 2:45

Prayer is a light,
charity is a proof
and patience
is luminous.

Hadith (Muslim)

Spill tears if
you have grief,
as tears of grief
provide relief.

Sha'wana

Patience is fighting all

that the *nafs** likes.

Sheikh Nazim Al-Haqqani

*nafs* meaning human ego
or the "lower" self

# THE PROPHETIC CHARACTER: PATIENCE

We live in an impatient world, and this can permeate our own character and behaviour, especially with the people we love the most. Who are you impatient with in your life? This Ramadan, set aside time to fix that. Dedicate meaningful and quality time to be with them, even if it's challenging.

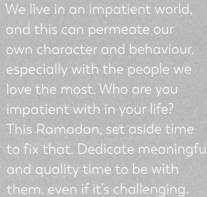

So remember
Me and I will
remember you.

Qur'an 2:152

# Be mindful of Allah and He will protect you.

**Hadith (at-Tirmidhi)**

What you give your
attention to is going to
determine your reality.

Sheikh Hamza Yusuf Hanson

I am a fountain,

You are my water.

I flow from You to You.

*Zeynep Hatun*

# Meditation on Mindfulness

The origins of the phrase "mindfulness" can be traced back to the Buddhist religious concept of "remembrance". For Muslims, mindfulness is to always be in a state of *dhikr* – remembrance of Allah (ﷻ). Try it, even for a few minutes, and see how that anchors you in the moment.

Do not do a favour
expecting more
in return.

Qur'an 74:6

# Verily, every person will have only what they intended.

Hadith (al-Bukhari)

Acting on one's knowledge
is not in the amount of
fasting, almsgiving and
praying that one does
[but] in sincerely dedicating
one's actions to God.

Al-Wahatiyya (Umm al-Fadl)

Try and remember the joy
that is the consequence
of sincere giving that
nobody knows about.

*Sheikh Abdal Hakim Murad*

# PURIFYING YOUR INTENTIONS

Allah (ﷻ) judges every action upon what is intended in our hearts. This Ramadan, reflect on the motives behind your actions and contributions. When you say or do things for others, are you expecting something in return? Or maybe you are giving to be seen as someone who is generous?

My mercy embraces
all things.

Qur'an 7:156

Allah has pardoned my nation for their mistakes, their forgetfulness and what they are coerced into doing.

**Hadith (Ibn Majah)**

There is no man who
is unable to repent and
start to live a useful life.

Shaikh Ali Nureddin
al-Yashruti al-Hassani
al-Husseini

The heaviest thing for the slave
[believer] is sinfulness, and
the lightest is repentance.

*Zubda (Umm Ali) of Baghdad*

# The Prophetic
# Character: Mercy for All

How can you embody mercy? We all
have opportunities to show mercy to
others. Mercy could be as grand as being
charitable with your wealth, or as simple
as helping a parent and child carry their
pushchair up some steps. Showing mercy
to others is easier than you think.

The life of this
world is no more
than the delusion
of enjoyment.

Qur'an 57:20

# Renounce the world and Allah will love you.

Hadith (Ibn Majah)

The fulfilment of the
heart is in rejection
of the world.

Futayma of Nishapur

Love has made me indifferent
to the world. In loving my Friend,
my life's breath has left me.

*Hasan Raja*

# A TIME FOR SECLUSION

It was during a period of seclusion and profound contemplation in Ramadan that the Prophet Muhammad (ﷺ) received divine revelations. This Ramadan, consider removing yourself from your everyday surroundings, even for a short while, and retreating to a place where you can also experience the wisdom and beauty of reflection in seclusion.

So do not oppress
the orphan, nor
repulse the beggar.

Qur'an 93:9–10

I have forbidden
injustice for Myself
and I have forbidden
it among you, so
do not oppress
one another.

**Hadith (Muslim)**

Allah does not forget
the pain of the wronged
one, the isolation of the
lonely one, nor the crime
of the oppressor.

Omar Suleiman

An interpretation of Islam that
is in harmony with equality
and democracy is an authentic
expression of faith.

*Shirin Ebadi*

# The Prophetic Character: Just

Being just is about treating all of Allah's (ﷻ) creations fairly, whether they are people, animals or plants. This means not allowing our conscious or unconscious biases to influence our behaviour. To be just, we need to examine our inner prejudices, identify our blind spots and confront our biases.

He elevated some of
you in rank over others,
so He may test you with
what He has given you.

Qur'an 6:165

None of you will have faith until he loves for his brother what he loves for himself.

Hadith (al-Bukhari)

God looked with favour
on a folk, and they stayed
away from worldly fortunes.

A'ishah al-Ba'uniyyah

A generous person may
not have wisdom: but,
unlike others, he has
the means to gain it.

*Idries Shah*

# THE TIME
# FOR GIVING

This is the month when we should look at our material wealth and consider how much of it we *really* need and how we could be more generous. During Ramadan, when Muslims across the globe are at their most charitable, try to give what you can. Generosity enriches both the giver and recipient.

You will never achieve
righteousness until
you donate some of
what you cherish.

Qur'an 3:92

Consult your soul,
consult your heart.
Righteousness is what
reassures your soul
and your heart.

**Hadith (al-Darimi)**

The Worker is concealed in
the workshop: go you and
seek Him there, for the work
has woven a net over Him.

Muhammad Marmaduke Pickthall

Whoever sets things
right with God, the whole
universe is theirs.

*Lady Nafisa*

# Meditation on Righteousness

Righteous is defined as being morally
correct or free from wrongdoing; to be
righteous then is intrinsically linked to
morality. As Muslims, our moral compass
is defined by the spirit of Islam. Take
the opportunity to explore this spirit
for yourself, allowing it to shape your
character and behaviour. Cultivating
this attitude will guide you
toward righteousness.

I am truly most forgiving to whoever repents, believes and does good, then persists on true guidance.

Qur'an 20:82

Follow a bad deed
with a good deed
and it will erase it,
and behave with
good character
toward people.

Hadith (at-Tirmidhi)

The intelligent person is one
who protects the interests
of his brothers, not one who
follows his brothers' desires.

Abu Sulayman al-Darani

Remember those in perennial fast,

constantly in hunger and deprivation,

Share with the poor, orphans

and the destitutes, to make

inclusive your celebration.

*Kazi Nazrul Islam*

# GIVING UP A VICE

Ramadan is a practical gift.
It serves as an annual cleanser,
prompting us to pause, take
stock and rein in any bad habits
we may have developed over
the past year. Use Ramadan
as an opportunity to weed
out vices. Resisting them
throughout the month might
inspire you to extend your
resolve beyond Ramadan.

So, surely with
hardship comes ease.

Qur'an 94:5

Verily Allah does
not look at your
appearance and
wealth, but rather
He looks at your heart
and your actions.

**Hadith (Muslim)**

The Almighty has made
each one of us unique and
there is only one of you.
Focus on being the best
version of yourself.

Mufti Menk

When light enters the heart,
darkness departs from it
andit is rightly guided.

*Nana Asma'u*

# Meditation on Hardship

Ramadan is a good time to put our hardships into perspective by reflecting on the trials endured by the Prophet (ﷺ). He was an orphan who suffered regular insults, who was initially disbelieved my many and rejected by his own tribe. His perseverance reminds us to find strength and resilience in the face of adversity.

I do not know
the precise moment when
the truth of Islam dawned
on me. It seems that I have
always been a Muslim.

Lady Zainab
Evelyn Cobbold

"Which religion is
the most beloved to
Allah?" The Prophet
said, "Pure, easy
monotheism."

Hadith (Ahmad)

Say, O Prophet, "We believe in Allah and what has been revealed to us and what was revealed to Abraham, Ishmael, Isaac, Jacob and his descendants; and what was given to Moses, Jesus and other prophets from their Lord – we make no distinction between any of them, and to Him we fully submit."

Qur'an 3:84

As soon as we become fully aware
that God exists, and thereupon
surrender ourselves to Him both
in faith and in our attitudes, we
fulfil the meaning of our life.

*Muhammad Asad*

# THE PROPHETIC CHARACTER: RESPECT

Islam is not a new religion; it is built on the same foundations previous religions were built upon, particularly Christianity and Judaism. It is also commonly believed that many messengers were sent to communities not explicitly mentioned in religious texts. Be mindful then that the wisdom you follow may exist in unexpected places, so it's important to respect the beliefs of others.

Eat and drink but
do not waste. Surely
He does not like
the wasteful.

Qur'an 7:31

Moses said: "Who are the poorest of Your servants?"

Allah said: "Those who desire more than they need."

**Hadith (Ibn Hibban)**

Waste not your Hour,
nor in the vain pursuit
Of This and That
endeavour and dispute.

Omar Khayyam

We know that one day, there will be full accountability before God; in the meantime, we continue to seek accountability on earth.

*Dr Ingrid Mattson*

# To Feast or to Fast?

During Ramadan, you may receive many *iftar* invitations and encounter an abundance of delicious food. It is sometimes easy to fall into excess during a month that is all about restraint. Ramadan is about the fast and not the feast. Be mindful of this and see if you can carry this lesson forward into life when the blessed month passes.

◆

Once you make a decision, put your trust in Allah. Surely Allah loves those who trust in Him.

Qur'an 3:159

If you have sins
piling up to the
clouds and then ask
for My forgiveness,
I will forgive you
without hesitation.

Hadith (at-Tirmidhi)

Let every tongue this truth
declare, and every life attest,
There's but one God,
He has no peer,
Till from North,
South and West.

Amina Emily Lincoln

Before one comes to the
real conception of God,
the first thing is to build
Him in one's heart.

Hazrat Inayat Khan

## OBEDIENCE TO ALLAH

During Ramadan, as we exercise self-discipline and appreciate the wisdom behind its demands, consider other ways you could be more obedient to Allah (). Write down five possibilities, and next to each option identify a practical way to achieve it. Use this month to put these ideas into practice.

Those who do good
will have the finest
reward and even more.

Qur'an 10:26

You must have
good character
and observe long
periods of silence.

**Hadith (al-Bazzar)**

When something does go the way you choose, you should know that it is going the way Allah Almighty chooses.

Shaykh Muhammad al-Yaqoubi

What you do in your
good time, will come to
you in your difficult time.

*Dr Haifaa Younis*

# Do More Good

Doing good things is easier than you might think. Set yourself the goal of achieving one big and one small act of kindness each week during Ramadan. Keep these realistic and attainable. It might be practical help for a family member alongside something simpler, like rounding up a weekly payment and donating that difference to charity.

Humanity was
once nothing but a
single community.

Qur'an 10:19

You have no virtue
over one with white
skin or black skin,
except by favour of
righteousness.

Hadith (Ahmad)

Today, the person who
speaks the truth and the
person who is aware of
God finds himself in
a wave-tossed sea.

Fatima al-Nisaburiya

The most knowledgeable
of people is the one with
the most knowledge of
people's differences.

*Imam Abu Hanifa*

# TACKLE YOUR IGNORANCE

We all have areas where we lack knowledge or understanding. This Ramadan, why not take the opportunity to learn about a culture or a group of people you have always been ignorant of. Better still, consider exploring one that you frequently encounter but know very little about.

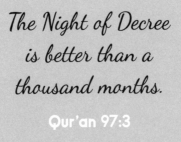

The Night of Decree
is better than a
thousand months.

Qur'an 97:3

Whoever stands
in prayer during the
Night of Decree
due to faith and
seeking reward, his
previous sins will
be forgiven.

**Hadith (al-Bukhari)**

It is through prayer that the
service of God is acquired.

Hazrat Khwaja
Moinuddin Hasan Chisti

Reason can take
you to His door, but
only His grace can
take you beyond.

*Sanai Ghaznavi*

# Meditation on Grace

Grace when discussed in the context of
the Divine relates to Allah's (ﷻ) approval
or kindness. During this blessed month, as
we engage in self-reflection, remember to
be grateful for where Allah (ﷻ) has shown
you kindness. Ponder which aspects of
your life would Allah (ﷻ) approve
of, and what might not align with
Allah's (ﷻ) favour.

◆

When I get tired
of human encounter,
I find intimacy in the
remembrance of God.

Lubaba al-Muta Abbida

The five daily *salat*
(prayers), Friday (prayer)
to the next Friday
(prayer) and the fasting
of Ramadan is expiation
of the sins committed.

Hadith (Muslim)

If human beings communicated with their *fitra*\*, it would lead them to the fulfilment of their soul's longing, to life according to the Law of creation.

Aisha Rafea

\**fitra* meaning innate nature or primordial disposition

The objective of asceticism is to leave all that harms the servant's Hereafter and the objective of worship is to do all that will benefit his Hereafter.

*Ibn Taymiyyah*

# PURIFYING
# THE SOUL

Purifying the soul is a process of self-reflection and inner growth. Practices that can support this journey include: cultivating a habit of performing good deeds; having integrity; being just; surrounding yourself with positive influence; taking responsibility for your actions; accepting your mistakes; being kind; caring for others; responding with forgiveness; being charitable (with your wealth, time and behaviour).

Do not let the hatred of a people lead you to injustice. Be just! That is closer to righteousness.

**Qur'an 5:8**

I love God: I have no
time left in which
to hate the devil.

**Rabi'a al-Adawiyya**

Many of the faults you
see in others, dear reader,
are your own nature
reflected in them.

Rumi

What waves of understanding and
compassion would follow if we
stood in one another's shoes.

*Queen Rania Al Abdullah
of Jordan*

# The Prophetic Character: Empathy

Understanding and sharing the feelings of others can be difficult for many people. To cultivate empathy, try shifting your focus toward the people around you. Practice active listening; avoid making conversations self-centred and reflect before you respond to someone. Don't dismiss views just because you disagree. Imagine yourself in another person's shoes and validate their feelings instead of minimizing them.

*Allah is with those who restrain themselves.*

Qur'an 16:128

Whoever does not
leave evil words and
deeds while fasting,
Allah does not need
him to leave food
and drink.

Hadith (al-Bukhari)

I am the traveller who has
experienced the weight
of too much baggage.

Tahereh Saffarzadeh

Do not be proud if you have been devout, thinking that you have brought any present to the hall of royal audience.

*Saadi Shirazi*

## WHICH PILLAR TO IMPROVE

Most Muslims consider five pillars key to their religious practice: declaration of faith; prayer; fasting during Ramadan; Hajj; charity. While you focus on Ramadan, have you considered focusing on another pillar as well? Maybe you can start planning for Hajj, improve your observance of daily prayers, or learn how to calculate your annual charitable obligation.

Whoever of you is ill
or on a journey, then let
them fast an equal number
of days after Ramadan.

**Qur'an 2:185**

Whoever eats and drinks forgetfully while he is fasting, let him complete his fast, for Allah has fed him and given him drink.

**Hadith (al-Bukhari)**

He who would know the
secrets of both worlds,
Will find the secret of
them both, is Love.

Attar of Nishapur

Ours is a materialistic age,

but there are those

who follow the Way.

*Sayyida Fatima*

# Unnecessary Hardship

This Ramadan, be mindful that observing it doesn't require being harsh on yourself. If circumstances arise like travel, illness, pregnancy or health problems, remember there is no obligation to fast. So don't feel guilty or self-conscious; Islam is not meant to impose unnecessary difficulty on you.

◆

Whoever saves a life,
it will be as if they saved
the whole of humanity.

Qur'an 5:32

I have prepared
for My righteous
servants what no eye
has seen, what no ear
has heard and what no
heart has perceived.

Hadith (al-Bukhari)

This is what my soul is
telling me: be peaceful
and love everyone.

Malala Yousafzai

Make our hearts the seats of
mercy and love, and make them
in Thy thought for ever more.

*Muhammad Iqbal*

## MONTH OF FORGIVENESS

We have all held onto a grudge for too long; sometimes without the source of our grudge even being aware of it. In this month of forgiveness, reflect and consider who you need to forgive (including yourself) to move forward and make amends.

Allah does not require
of any soul more than
what it can afford.

**Qur'an 2:286**

No one leaves their
house in search of
knowledge but that
the angels will lower
their wings in approval
of what he does.

**Hadith (Ibn Majah)**

Education is our passport
to the future, for tomorrow
belongs only to the people
who prepare for it today.

Malik el-Shabbazz
AKA Malcolm X

Though spirituality, silence and meditation leave one with a sense of extreme beauty and comfort, staying there is ignoring our realities as human beings.

*Zainab Salbi*

# Stand for Something

We all have a sphere of concern and a sphere of influence. In the first, we can be concerned about things knowing we cannot impact them directly. In the second, we realize we can influence the outcome of something. As Ramadan comes to an end, think about what you can influence for good.

There is nothing like Him,
for He alone is the
All-Hearing All-Seeing.

Qur'an 42:11

Fasting is a shield,
charity extinguishes
sins as water
extinguishes fire.

Hadith (at-Tirmidhi)

If you give a poor person money, before it drops into his or her hand, it falls into God's hands.

Hatice Cenan Hanim

In every blade of grass I see

Thy sacred loving hand;

In every thought that comes to me,

Behold the Promised Land.

*Saif-ur-Rahman Rahmatullah*
*Farooq Lord Headley*

# THE PROPHETIC CHARACTER: GRATITUDE

As Muslims, we acknowledge that everything is from Allah (ﷻ), but let us not forget to show gratitude to Allah's (ﷻ) "instruments". Say "thank you" to your parents more for their sacrifices, your friends for their support, your colleagues for their assistance, the taxi driver for getting you home safely, and even your pet for their affectionate presence.

The true servants of
the Most Compassionate
are those who walk on
the earth humbly.

**Qur'an 25:63**

# Call upon Me, I will respond to you.

**Qur'an 40:60**

The people think of wealth
and power as the greatest fate,
But in this world, a spell of
health is the best state.

Sultan Suleiman
the Magnificent

Be the person you want
to be, and the world
can change for you.

*Stephanie Kurlow*

# The Prophetic Character: Humility

Humans by nature are egocentric, but there are certain traits that can help us develop humility. Take responsibility for your actions and say sorry in a meaningful way. Be open to feedback from everyone. Avoid boasting. Admit when you're wrong and someone else is right. Show appreciation toward others. Most importantly, do all of these with sincerity.

He has perfect
knowledge of
all things.

Qur'an 57:3

Whoever travels
a path in search of
knowledge, Allah will
make easy for him a
path to Paradise.

**Hadith (Muslim)**

Why do we not hear? If we
hear the sound of the words,
why do we not understand?
If we understand, why do
we not act accordingly?

Sâmiha Ayverdi

There is no greater wealth than
wisdom, no greater poverty
than ignorance.

*Ali ibn Abu Talib*

# IMPROVING ISLAMIC KNOWLEDGE

This Ramadan, take a moment to reflect on areas where you can enhance your knowledge of Islam. Consider reading the entire Qur'an in a language you feel comfortable with, or delving into the *Seerah*\* of the Prophet (ﷺ). Perhaps you could explore the rich history of Islamic communities through the ages. Embrace this opportunity to deepen your understanding.

\**Seerah* meaning the life story of Prophet Muhammad (ﷺ). The *Seerah* provides a comprehensive understanding of the Prophet's (ﷺ) character and his mission

He is truly
the Most Kind,
the Most Merciful.

**Qur'an 52:28**

Allah is gentle, and
He loves gentleness. He
rewards for gentleness
what is not granted
for harshness, and
He does not reward
anything else like it.

**Hadith (Muslim)**

Let us be lovers and
loved ones. The world
shall be left to no one.

Yunus Emre

I take love as my religion wherever
its caravans lead, for love is
my religion and my faith.

*Ibn Arabi*

# Show More Love

The Qur'an teaches us to love one another
and embody kindness and compassion.
So, how can you show more genuine,
unconditional love? Consider how you can
express more love to your parents, children
or spouse. What about your friends, teachers,
or those you encounter in everyday life,
like waitstaff, cashiers or delivery drivers?
Remember, love is the essence of creation.

Have you enjoyed this book?
If so, find us on Facebook at
**Summersdale Publishers**, on Twitter at
**@Summersdale** and on Instagram and
TikTok at **@summersdalebooks** and get
in touch. We'd love to hear from you!

## www.summersdale.com

## Image Credits